Lucy and the Enchanted Valentine

Written by
J.P. Anthony Williams

Lucy loved Valentine's Day. She spent hours at her craft table, cutting, gluing, and drawing on colorful paper to make the perfect valentine cards for her friends and family.

As she worked on her favorite card, she accidentally cut out a heart-shaped hole in the middle.
"Oh no!" Lucy sighed, holding up the card. Suddenly, the hole started to glow with a soft pink light.

"What's happening?" Lucy whispered as the light grew brighter. Before she could blink, the hole turned into a magical portal.
A gentle voice called out, "Come through, Lucy. The Land of Hearts needs you!"

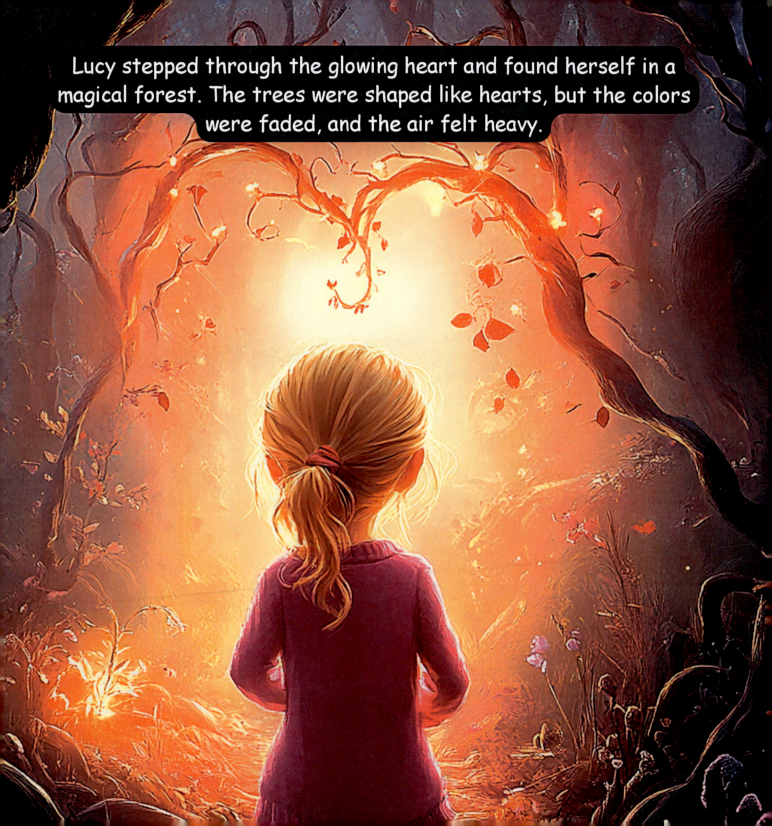

She saw a grand palace in the distance and decided to follow the path toward it.

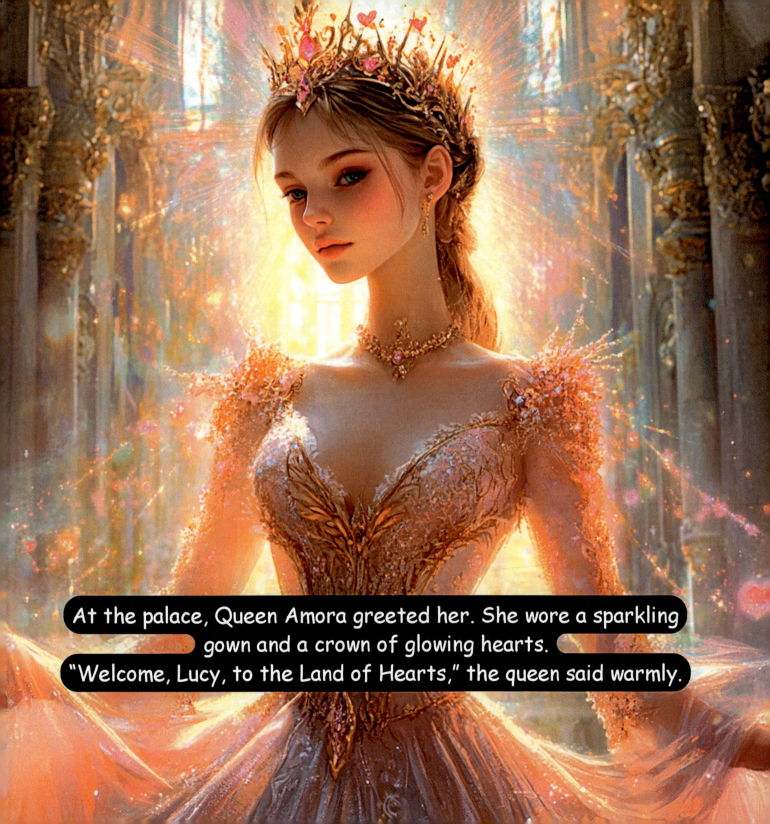

At the palace, Queen Amora greeted her. She wore a sparkling gown and a crown of glowing hearts.
"Welcome, Lucy, to the Land of Hearts," the queen said warmly.

Lucy looked around at the faded palace. "What is this place? And why does everything look so gray and sad?"

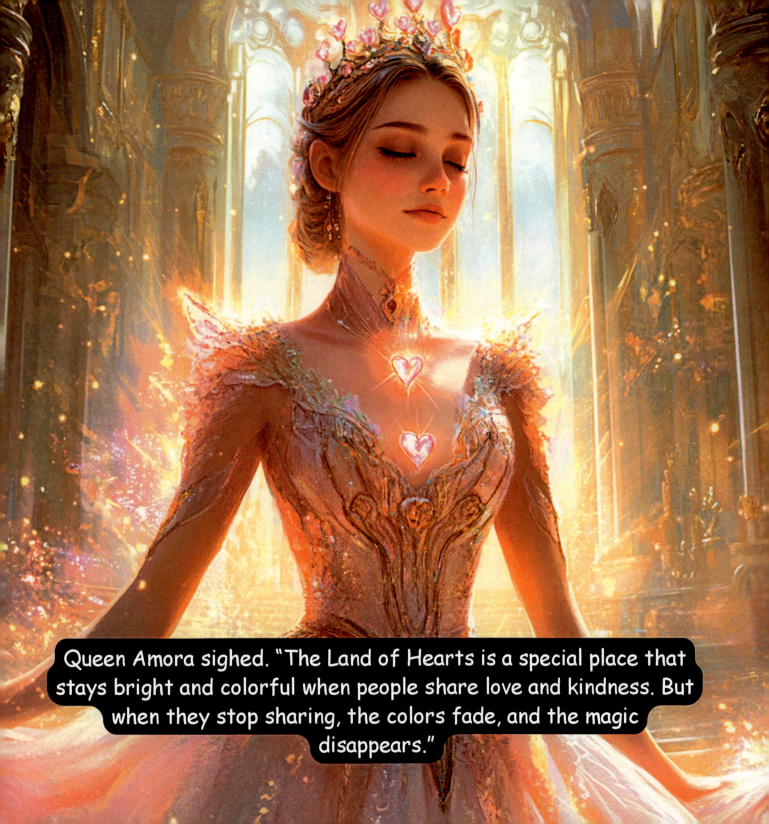

Queen Amora sighed. "The Land of Hearts is a special place that stays bright and colorful when people share love and kindness. But when they stop sharing, the colors fade, and the magic disappears."

Lucy's eyes widened. "That's so sad."
The queen smiled. "Will you help us bring back the colors by sharing love and kindness?"
Lucy nodded. "I'll do my best!"

Lucy walked into a gloomy forest clearing where the trees were bare, and the ground was cracked. She saw Benny the Bunny sitting sadly under a tree.

"But you didn't tell me!" Benny said. "I thought you didn't care about our friendship anymore."

Lucy smiled. "Benny, maybe Sally didn't know how to explain. Sally, maybe Benny just misses spending time with you."

Sally nodded. "I'm sorry, Benny. I should have told you."
Benny smiled. "I'm sorry too. I didn't know you were so busy."

Next, Lucy entered a quiet garden where the ground was dry, and no flowers were growing. Rosie the Robin flapped her wings nervously. "Hi, my name is Rosie and I've been trying to plant seeds of kindness, but it's too much for one bird," she said.

Lucy spotted Holly the Hedgehog nearby. "Why don't you help Rosie?" Lucy asked.
"I'd like to," Holly said shyly, "but I'm afraid my spines will ruin the seeds."

Lucy smiled. "Your spines might actually be perfect for this!" Holly cautiously used her spines to poke tiny holes in the soil. Rosie dropped seeds into each hole, and Lucy helped cover them with dirt and water.

As they worked together, the garden came alive! Flowers of every color blossomed, filling the air with a sweet scent. Holly beamed. "I didn't know I could be so helpful!"

Rosie chirped, "Thank you, Holly and Lucy. The garden is beautiful again!"

Lucy walked further and reached a tall tower wrapped in darkness. Fireflies buzzed around it, glowing faintly.

"Timmy the Turtle is supposed to light the tower," one firefly explained, "but he's too scared to come out of his shell."

Lucy knelt down. "It's okay to be slow. Everyone moves at their own pace. What matters is that you're brave enough to try." Timmy peeked out of his shell. "Do you really think so?"

"I know so," Lucy said with a smile. Timmy slowly climbed to the top of the tower. The fireflies cheered, and their glow became brighter and brighter. The entire tower lit up, spreading warmth and light across the land.

Lucy returned to the palace, where Queen Amora was waiting. The Land of Hearts was now bursting with color and joy.

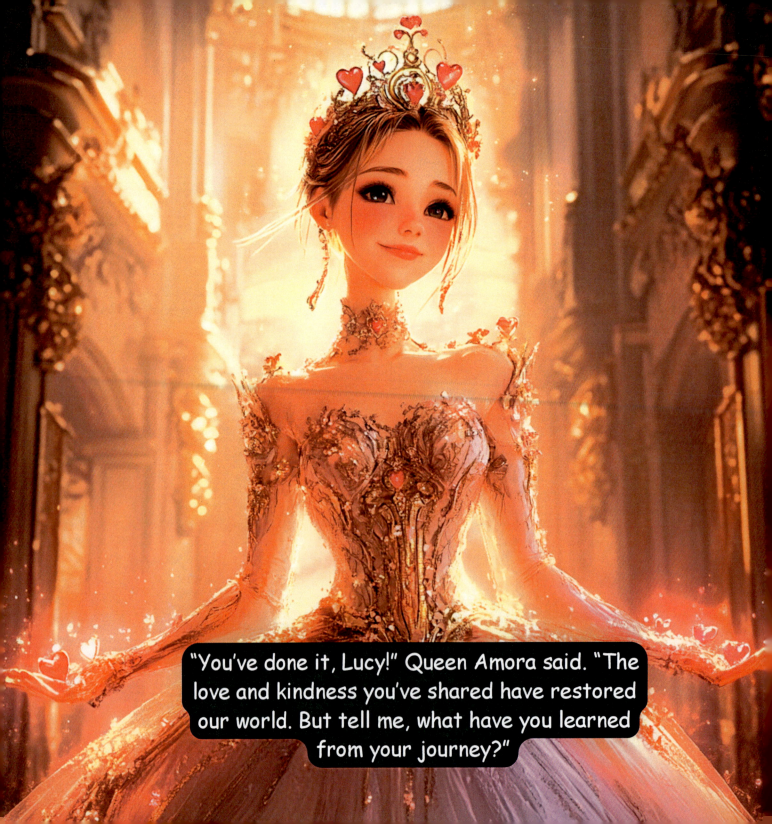

"You've done it, Lucy!" Queen Amora said. "The love and kindness you've shared have restored our world. But tell me, what have you learned from your journey?"

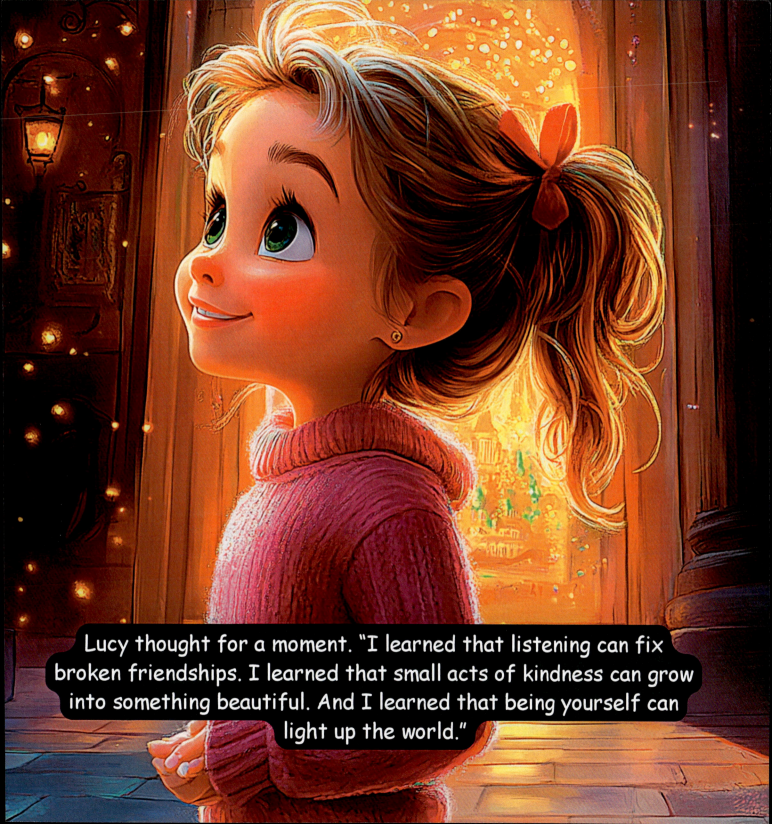

Lucy thought for a moment. "I learned that listening can fix broken friendships. I learned that small acts of kindness can grow into something beautiful. And I learned that being yourself can light up the world."

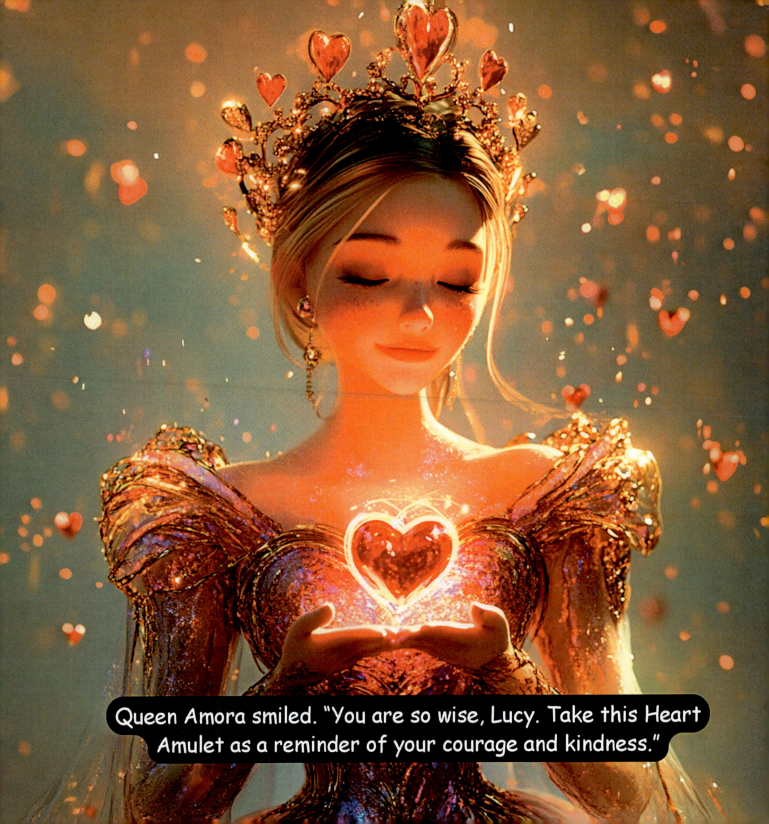

Queen Amora smiled. "You are so wise, Lucy. Take this Heart Amulet as a reminder of your courage and kindness."

Thank You - Your Free Gift

Thank you for reading **"Lucy and the Enchanted Valentine"**

I hope you enjoyed it and if you have a minute to spare, I would be extremely grateful if you could post <u>a short review on my book's Amazon page</u>

To show my gratitude, I am offering a **FREE** copy of this amazing <u>Animals Coloring Book.</u> Download your free copy by clicking on the link below

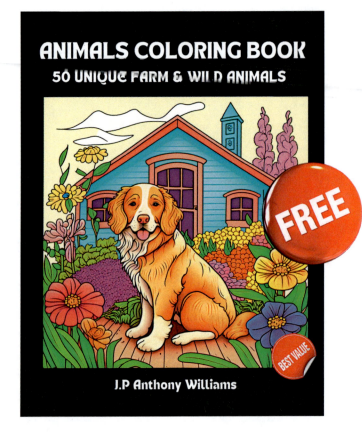

What's Next
Scan the QR code to check out the other books in this Series

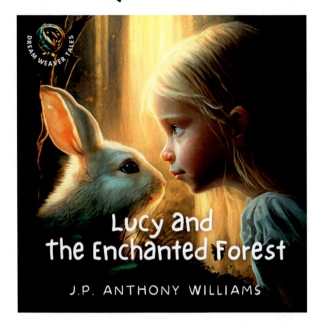

Scan me

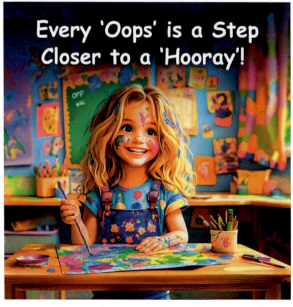

What's Next

Scan the QR code to check out the other books in this Series

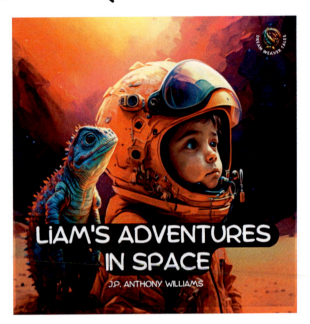

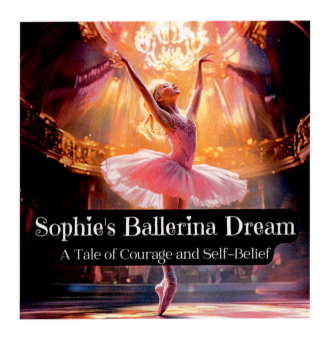

What's Next

Scan the QR code to check out the other books in this Series

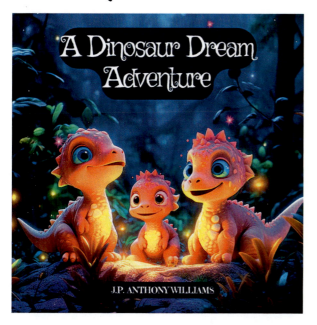
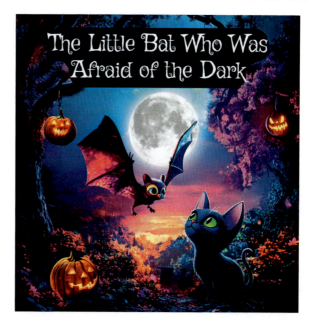
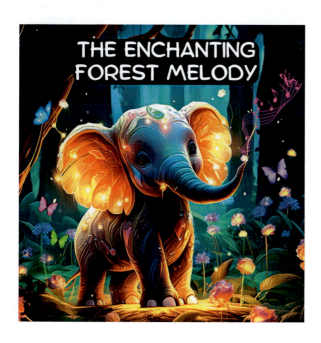

What's Next

Scan the QR code to check out the other books in this Series

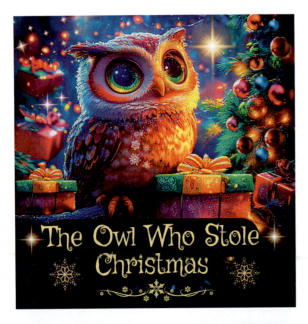

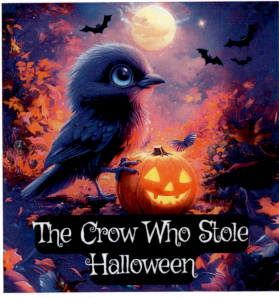

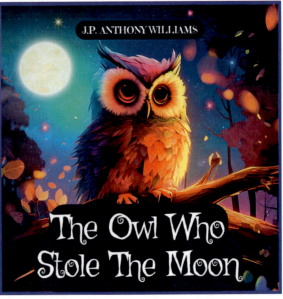

The world of J.P. Anthony Williams

About the Author

J.P Anthony Williams is a bestselling children's book author, known for his enchanting tales and vivid illustrations. His stories are loved by young readers all over the world.

Born and raised in a small town, J.P developed a love of nature and storytelling at an early age. He spent his childhood exploring the woods and fields near his home, and he loved nothing more than curling up with a good book.

J.P's stories are known for their vivid imagery and richly-detailed illustrations. He takes inspiration from the natural world and from the myths and legends of his childhood, and he weaves them into tales that are both entertaining and educational.

In his free time, J.P can be found exploring new places and seeking inspiration for his next book. He is also a big advocate for environmental conservation, and often uses his platform to raise awareness about nature and its preservation.

Copyright © 2024 by J.P. Anthony Williams

All rights reserved. This book or any portion thereof may not be reproduced or used in any manner whatsoever without the express written permission of the author.

Made in United States
North Haven, CT
08 February 2025